handwritten: To: Ann

Ten
Commandments
of
Leadership
Networking

by

Eddy Ketchersid

handwritten: God Bless You Real Good!

handwritten signature: Bro, Eddy Ketchersid 10/3/08

Ketch Publishing

Eddy Ketchersid-Community Minister
Farmers Branch Church of Christ
3035 Valley View Ln. Farmers Branch, TX 75234
972-247-2109 E-Mail broeddy@thebranch.org
Cell 972-345-1645

ISBN 978-0-9801420-1-3

Ketch
Publishing

4675 N. Benton Dr.
Bloomington, Indiana 47408

www.KetchPublishing.com

CONTENTS

TO MY FAMILY AND ASSOCIATES

Verlen, my loving wife for fifty years and the mother of our six children, is my business partner and CFO. She has proofread all my manuscripts and given expert counsel in the compilation of this book. To her I owe a debt that can never be repaid!

Our oldest son, Allen, through his publishing company, has encouraged and guided the layout, art work and production of this volume. His own prolific gift of writing and academic scholarship are well known in various circles. I am honored to have him partner with me in this publication. President Woodrow Wilson was right when he said, *"We should not only use all the brains we have --- but all that we can borrow."*

I am grateful to our Lord for bringing around me some the finest people in the world. Several of them are named in this volume. May His continuing blessing be upon each one!

Eddy Ketchersid

PS Please checked the back pages of this book for a listing of those who have heard some or all of these *Ten Commandments of Leadership Networking*.

Endorsements:

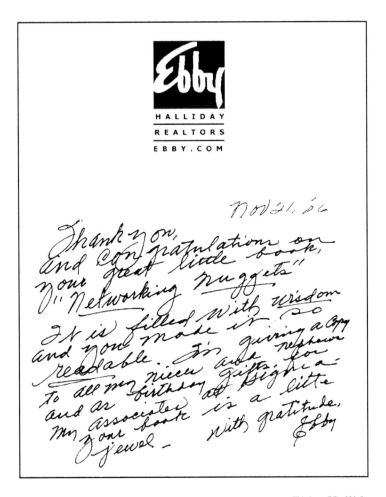

Nov 21, 06

Thank you,
and Congratulations on
your great little book,
"Networking Nuggets"
It is filled with wisdom
and you made it so
readable. I'm giving a copy
to all my nieces and nephews
and as a birthday gift for
my associates at Highland
Your book is a little
jewel - with gratitude,
Ebby

Ebby Halliday
Halliday Realtors

"As a former FedEx Global Sales Manager and a current entrepreneur, I have found Eddy Ketchersid's timely advice on networking to be invaluable. We leverage his keen insight to build stronger bonds with our multinational clients and open new doors to professional relationships. The Ten Commandments of Networking are priceless reminders of the power of Godly principles applied in every corner of our lives. Thank you Eddy for opening our eyes - and accelerating our success!"

Keith Martino
President, College Market Institute

"We are privileged to have the OPPORTUNITY to watch Bro. Eddy Ketchersid work his "Magic" and enrich our lives at our weekly Networking Group Session! He is absolutely amazing!!!! YOU will cherish this book!"

Fred Ferguson,
President
Farmers Branch Chamber of Commerce

"Eddy Ketchersid's people skills have been honed to perfection from his many years of public service. He is without peer as an ambassador of goodwill for our community."

Ben Robinson
Farmers Branch City Councilman

"A book is only as great as its author. Having known Bro Eddy Ketchersid for almost 20 years I consider him to be a great man. I have benefited so much from his networking knowledge."

C.W. Lowrimore
This is the day the Lord has made.
Tex-Tenn Transporters

"The Ten Commandments of Leadership Networking encompasses the basic ways to maximize your networking. Sometimes, we forget some important components and this just "hits it home". These are good rules to just live with day-by-day as we conduct business and life in general. Thank you so much for sharing your expertise and wisdom."

Joyce Nissen
Hilton Hotels

"I have known Eddy Ketchersid as a minister, master speaker and effective business leader. In these capacities, Eddy has shared his lessons learned from a lifetime of teaching with literally thousands of people. Until now, his message has been limited to public speaking engagements, but through Ten Commandments of Leadership Networking, Eddy casts the net even wider. I am a better person because of my affiliation with Eddy Ketchersid and after reading this book, you will be too."

John Land
President of the Frisco Chamber of Commerce

The <u>Ten Commandments of Leadership Networking</u> is a comfort to me because the elements of living in the real dog-eat-dog world of business is a troubling issue for many Christians. With this program you get a minister's touch with practical guide for living our faith out in the world where mercy is hard-coming, and grace is lacking.

Don Braugh
Carrollton, TX

Your first book, "Networking Nuggets" has been invaluable to our Farmers Branch Chamber of Commerce members. Your Networking tips are very informative, interesting and best of all, They WORK!!!!

You literally "own" the room when You present them to our weekly Branch Out Meeting. Your Networking Tips are a "Wonderment"!

What an ASSET you are to our Community and Chamber. You have opened our minds' eyes to a better way of doing business and we enjoy our lives more because of you!

Fred Ferguson, President
Farmers Branch Chamber of Commerce

Eddy Ketchersid knows Leadership Networking! Ketchersid has done a magnificent job getting to the core of what it takes to be a great networker. <u>Ten Commandments of Leadership Networking</u> will challenge you to rethink and reinvent the way you project yourself and your business in the marketplace. It is a must read for anyone looking to hone their networking skills and get their message across in a meaningful and memorable way.

Jason O'Quinn
President, Petra Lending Group
Dallas, Texas

The Ten Commandments of Leadership principles provide the framework necessary to become a successful leader and how to make every networking opportunity work for you. Eddy Ketchersid has enriched the lives of so many in this community through his leadership and training.

Lara Orlic
Director of Chamber Relations
Farmers Branch Chamber of Commerce

The most important lesson from these Ten Commandments is never assume or take anything for granted when it comes to networking opportunities. Bro. Eddy is right on target with each Commandment. Each lesson equips you professionally to make your networking efforts stand out in every situation and add to your success in business.

Richard Brown
New York Life Insurance Company
Farmers Branch, Texas

Eddy is always on the cutting edge when it comes to Networking and Leadership. His "commandments" are extremely useful both in and out of the work place. Eddy has a heart of gold and will certainly get you moving in the right direction.

Scott Garner
Radio & Television Broadcaster
Frisco RoughRiders Baseball Club

I have heard many of the Ten Commandants that Bro. Eddy has written about and I have applied several of them to my day-to-day business affairs. I must say that the one that sticks out the most is "Always be a Host." This has changed the way I approach my customers, my networking groups and my work. Thank you for this simple yet valuable commandant - I now look at every day as chance to serve.

Tammi Burgee
Sales and Marketing Manager
Fidelity National Home Warranty

Eddy Ketchersid not only talks the talk, but walks the walk. I cannot think of a person with more experience, wisdom and insight in leadership and networking. This book is an invaluable tool that will benefit everyone from the recent college grad to the CEO of a Fortune 500 company.

Tim O'Hare
O'Hare & Associates, Attorneys at Law
Mayor Pro Tem, City of Farmers Branch, Texas

Foreword

You can pick up any big, thick book in the bookstore and think, "Wow, this guy has done a lot of research and writing." But you may or may not be all that convinced that wading through it all is going to be worth the time and effort required. A good number of such books simply will not be worth the trouble.

I've done enough interior book layouts and cover designs to know full well that not every book with a pretty cover and fancy interior can even begin to deliver on the promising attractiveness of its appearance. All the artwork and expertise is on the surface of a great many books rolling off the presses these days. What you want, and need, is valuable material that is easily accessible and that will pay off for *you*, rather than simply beautifying your bookshelf. This will be a book that delivers real, practical value to you.

The Ten Commandments for Leadership Networking will convey to you very succinctly ten imperatives for successfully relating to people in your business and community interactions. Eddy Ketchersid *has* put in his time in researching the topic of networking and relationship building. But more importantly, he has over 50 years of experience in leadership and networking. He has quite intentionally built an untold number of longstanding and productive relationships over the course of his career. This is his forte. What he recommends works. He has done it, and is doing it, successfully.

Allen Ketchersid
Ketch Publishing

WAYS THIS BOOK
CAN HELP YOU

The last few years the publishing houses at home and abroad have printed millions of books relating to success in business. Most of them are filled with theory that does not answer the bottom line question, *"yes, but how?"*

Thus my justification for writing yet another book about success in leadership and networking skills is to make a *"yes, but how?"* contribution. Almost everyone understands the need, the question is *"how"* does one meet the need?

I gradually realized that I was sorely lacking in *"know how"* myself. As I look back across the years, I am appalled at my own frequent lack of finesse and understanding. There were no college courses, nor higher education classes in people skills and dealing successfully with people relationships. All research agrees that about fifteen percent of one's financial success is due to one's technical knowledge and about eighty-five percent is due to one's ability to lead people... personality ... attitude ... understanding communication ... building relationships.

The formulation of the ten simple but powerful statements contained in this book, started in 1995 with the encouragement of John Land, who was then the President of the Farmers Branch Chamber of Commerce. Once a month I compiled a new idea of leadership into *"A Leadership Commandment"*, later to be known as *"Ten Commandments of Leadership Networking"*. These principles were so strong, we came to call them COMMANDMENTS, because they were much more important than mere suggestions. We were convinced that in areas of leadership, they were *"to die for"* they were so vital!

I have presented *"Ten Commandments of Leadership Networking"* to Branch Out, the business networking group of the Farmers Branch Chamber of Commerce three times over a period of twelve years. They have been presented to other Chambers including Midland, Frisco, Plano, and many other networking groups, churches, management teams and organizations. These COMMANDMENTS really work!

In this book you are given the meat of my presentations and a brief outline which is to be duplicated and handed out. If you find these COMMANDMENTS helpful, and want to present them to your organization or staff, you have my permission to duplicate and share this material.

1. You will learn by *doing*!
   People skills can be developed only by *practicing* them.

2. Structure a schedule for practicing these *COMMANDMENTS* that fits your lifestyle.

   ➤ Take one *COMMANDMENT* a week/month and focus on practicing it.

   ➤ Teach the *COMMANDMENT* to others during that time.
   * Always give your hearers a handout copy of the *COMMANDMENT*.

   ➤ Walk the talk! Practice what you teach!

   ➤ Require accountability and measure progress.
   * Give your testimony about your own results.
   * Let others share their story in practicing the *COMMANDMENT*.

   ➤ Reward yourself and those you are coaching as you see improvement.

"Success seems to be connected with action. Successful people keep moving. They make mistakes, but they don't quit."

Conrad Hilton, *hotelier*

3. SUCCESS IS ABOUT CHOICES!

"In the long run, we shape our lives and we shape ourselves. The process never ends until we die. And the choices we make are ultimately our own responsibility."

Eleanor Roosevelt, *first lady*

Introduction

All of life has taught us that some things are more important than others. As infants we heard "No, no!" about things we were not to touch or play with. As we grew up, our parents taught us that chores, education and homework must have priority over idleness and entertainment. Leadership and successful business practices require priorities as well.

What is most important in networking and leadership?

What should take priority?

Biographies of the great men and women all draw us to the same conclusion. The most important accomplishments in life are possible only through healthy and strong RELATIONSHIPS.

What ever our goals may be, they always revolve around people and our relationships with them.

Thus these TEN COMMANDMENTS OF LEADERSHIP NETWORKING are about building successful relationships. They are about people skills and connecting constructively with others.

There is a basic fact about continuing success! Here it is:

Generally speaking,
people do business with those they…
KNOW, LIKE, and TRUST!

For people to KNOW you, LIKE you and TRUST you, positive relationships must occur.

These TEN COMMANDMENTS will lead you to develop the most needed people skills known to mankind for successful interaction with others.

COMMANDMENT #1

Always a host, never a guest.

SERVICE

A LEADER'S _FIRST_ COMMANDMENT

"Always a HOST, Never a GUEST"

As we begin the first commandment let's define two simple leadership terms. Webster's Unabridged Dictionary defines "GUEST" as a person who is entertained at the home or business of another, a person receiving hospitality where he or she is not a member. And, the dictionary defines "HOST or HOSTESS" as one who entertains quests either at home or away, at his own expense. Thus the guest and the host are almost opposites. Somewhat like hot and cold, daylight and dark, sweet and sour ... the guest and the host are quiet different.

THE CONTEXT

In the context of being a leader, networking and building relationships there is great power in this first commandment, _"ALWAYS A HOST, NEVER A GUEST"_. One's effectiveness in reaping great benefit from this commandment is largely based on attitude.

When Albert Schweitzer was awarded the Nobel Peace Prize in 1952, he stated, _"I don't know what your destiny will be, but one thing I do know; the only ones among you who will be really happy are those who have sought and found HOW TO SERVE."_

MIND SET

The best of all teachers has taught us, *"The greatest among you will be your SERVANT."* *(Matthew 23:11)* Being a servant and rendering service of a host is a mind set, but so is the opposite.

The "GUEST" mind set is a frame of mind which feels:

- I am here to receive hospitality, to be waited on, served and entertained.
- I will wait for directions and an invitation to participate.
- I will wait to be introduced.
- I will be passive and wait to be acted upon.

The "HOST" mind set is like Rotary International's motto, *"SERVICE ABOVE SELF":*

- I am here to give hospitality and entertain guests and others.
- I receive and accept others by taking responsibility toward them.
- I introduce myself to others, and then introduce them to others.
- I take the lead in starting conversation and circulate to include others.
- I initiate participation with friendliness and enthusiasm.
- I feel responsible to increase everyone's comfort and acceptance.

- I will be appropriately outgoing.
- I will be a compliment to the occasion by serving the occasion and others.

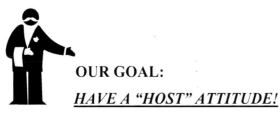

OUR GOAL:

HAVE A "HOST" ATTITUDE!

At any event that fits the context for "Leadership Networking" our goal is to practice the first commandment by having a "HOST" attitude. This does not mean that we will usurp the place of those who have organized the gathering. We are not present to seize the place of those sponsoring the event. Rather, we will compliment, honor, help, assist and facilitate the occasion toward its intended success.

Having a "HOST" attitude does not mean that we would monopolize conversations and attention, but we will so stimulate everyone that our presence is a welcome and needed asset.

YES, BUT HOW?

➤ Keep in mind your role that as a "HOST" and not a "GUEST", you are present to serve.

➤ Work at it! You can't spell "Networking" without "work"! It will require mental, emotional and physical work. But, as the great football coach, Vince Lombardi said, *"The only place success comes before work is in the dictionary."*

NOW FOR THE "SWEARING IN"
OF THE "ALWAYS A HOST,
NEVER A GUEST" POSSE.

Please raise your right hand and repeat after me!

> ➢ **"Never again will I be saying,
> 'No one spoke to me!'"**

> ➢ **"Never again will I be waiting to be
> spoken to first!"**

"BECAUSE, I AM THE HOST!"

The one word

**that summarizes this
commandment is**

"SERVICE"!

ADDITIONAL WISDOM
FOR THE FIRST COMMANDMENT

ALWAYS A HOST,
NEVER A GUEST

"We see our customers as invited guests to a party, and we are the hosts. It is our job every day to make every important aspect of the customer experience a little bit better."

Jeff Bezos, *Amazon.com founder*

"Good habits are as addictive as bad habits ---
and a lot more rewarding."

Harvey Mackay, *entrepreneur*

"For even I, the Son of Man, came here not be served but to serve others."

Jesus, *Mark 10:45*

TEN COMMANDMENTS
OF LEADERSHIP NETWORKING

A LEADER'S
<u>FIRST</u> COMMANDMENT

"Always a HOST, Never a GUEST"

1. The "GUEST" mind set –
   - *To receive hospitality, to be waited on, served and entertained.*
   - *Waits for directions, to be introduced and invited to participate.*
   - *Is passive and waits to be "acted upon".*

2. The "HOST" mind set –
   - *Gives hospitality and entertains guests.*
   - *Receives others and takes responsibility toward them.*
   - *Introduces self and others.*
   - *Leads in relationship starters and circulates to "host" others.*
   - *Initiates participation with friendliness and enthusiasm.*
   - *Feels responsible to increase everyone's comfort and acceptance.*
   - *Is appropriately "outgoing".*
   - *Compliments the occasion by serving the occasion and others.*

Our Goal:
Have a "HOST" attitude!

- ➤ This does not mean you will usurp the place of those who have organized the gathering.

- ➤ Rather, you will compliment, honor, help, assist and facilitate the occasion toward success.

- ➤ This does not mean you will monopolize conversations and attention, but you will so stimulate everyone that your presence is a welcome and needed asset.

Now for "SWEARING IN", please raise your right hand!

- ➤ *"Never again will I be saying, 'No one spoke to me!'"*

- ➤ *"Never again will I be waiting to be spoken to first!"*

COMMANDMENT #2

Never Underestimate
The Applause of One.

SUPPORT

A LEADER'S
SECOND COMMANDMENT:

"NEVER UNDERESTIMATE THE APPLAUSE OF ONE"

The late Mary Kay Ash, who built one of the largest cosmetic companies in the world through direct sales, was a master motivator. She taught and practiced a semblance of this second commandment when she said:

> *"Everyone wants to be appreciated.*
> *So if you appreciate someone, don't keep it a secret."*

My wife, Verlen, and I have six married children, and they have given us twenty-five grandchildren. Christmas and Thanksgiving holidays are performance time for the grandchildren. We hear them recite poems, sing songs and act out skits. Our response in claps, shouts of approval and compliments are to them as important as an appearance at Texas Stadium with the Dallas Cowboys.

In fifty years of public service we have learned that nothing is more important to children or adults than sincere expressions of appreciation and support.

Please understand that leadership and networking require developing a close relationship with the person(s) essential to the achievement of your goals. But, how do you build a close relationship? We know people generally do business with those they know, like and trust, but how do you help people know, like and trust you?

Dale Carnegie (1888-1955) was among the first in modern times to teach the art of human relationships in answer to what he saw as the craving of men and women to be liked, appreciated and valued. He recognized that this longing is in all of us. In his widely circulated book, *How to Win Friends and Influence People*, first published in 1936, he was one of the first to state that the biggest challenge in business is *"dealing with people"*.

Over seventy years ago it was obvious that success was based on twenty-five percent product knowledge and seventy-five percent dealing effectively with people. This has not changed even with all the technological advancements of our time.

Technical skills and book knowledge alone are not sufficient for success. Successful people, no matter what their area of business may be, must master leadership skills and understand how to get along with people.

The challenge of getting along with others is as old as Cain and Abel!

Relationships, whether personal or business, have a mysterious quality. They are hard to understand, explain and predict. It's easy to make someone dislike you, yet one can not force others to like him or be his friend. One can however, develop specific skills and habits that will make it more likely that others will respond to him positively, like him better, value and trust his friendship.

HOW TO DEVELOP THE SKILLS
AND FORM THE HABITS

Join the *"A.E.E. CLUB"* – the **A**ppreciation, **E**ncouragement, **E**nthusiasm club!

Develop the skills and form the habits of:

- ➢ Expressing genuine interest in others and their concerns!
- ➢ Expressing appreciation for them and their accomplishments!
- ➢ Encouraging them in their pursuits!
- ➢ Enthusiastically help them discover their importance!

To become powerful in leadership and networking, master a wide range of human relations skills by investing time and effort in developing them! Doing so will pay you more dividends than almost any investment you can make.

"THE APPLAUSE OF ONE"

The applause of one calls you to be liberal with your:
>*Appreciation,*
>*Affirmation,*
>*Approbation,*
>*Acknowledgement,*
>*Admiration,*
>*Compliments,*
>*Esteem,*
>*Honor,*
>*Love,*
>*Praise,*
>*Recognition,*
>*Relishing,*
>*Respecting,*
>*Regarding,*
>   *and*
>*Treasuring another!*

Here you have a list of fifteen action words to stimulate your mind toward discovering the motivation for your own personal applause.

Follow these fifteen action words with seven *ACTION GUIDELINES!*

1) Train your mind to be a good finder and to search for things you can applaud about others.

2) Learn to express praise when it is not expected, even when there has been defeat, failure or loss.

3) Always remember that the deepest craving in human nature is the longing to be appreciated, according to Wm. James, accredited as the father of American Psychiatry.

4) Sincere admiration has the power to draw out the best in others, like polishing silver.

5) Your applause of others deposits a great sum in your "credibility account" with the honored individual and with all who support him/her.

6) Your praise inspires and fires emotional energy in the recipient.

7) Your applause takes what in excellent in others and gives you ownership with them as it increases their value and yours.

THE POWER OF "AN AUDIENCE OF ONE"

The second commandment, *"NEVER UNDER-ESTIMATE THE APPLAUSE OF ONE"*, is about your own personal applause. You are the "one"! Come to understand how powerful and important your applause is … whether verbal or literal!   I've seen this not only in grandchildren when to them the clapping of two grandparents is as big as a thundering multitude, but also in the renewed faces of those I've counseled who needed only to hear an affirming word from just one individual they could trust.

"Never underestimate the applause of one" – *BECAUSE:*

1. It's contagious! You do it and others will "CATCH IT"!

2. It gives others permission to applaud because you have "broken the ice".

3. Remember that clapping is the most ancient expression of approval and appreciation in the history of humanity in all cultures!

4. It sets the right example!

5. It reaches the heart of the one you're supporting and all who support him/her!

BE LIBERAL WITH PRAISE!

A one word summary for this commandment:

"SUPPORT"

ADDITIONAL HELP FOR JOB SEEKERS

THANK-YOU NOTES HELP LAND JOBS

Sending a thank-you note after an interview gives job hopefuls a definite edge.

So says a poll of 150 senior execs by *Accountemps,* a staffing service for accounting and finance professionals.

The survey found 88% of execs said that sending a thank-you note following an interview can boost a job seeker's chances. These execs also estimate that 49% of applicants fail to do so.

But more job candidates are following up. Execs say that 51% of the candidates they interview send thank-you notes afterward.

Execs, who do hiring have preferences in how they get thank-yous.

Fifty-two percent say they like handwritten notes, while 44% prefer e-mail. Three percent prefer both, while 1%, don't know.

(*Source* - Investors Business Daily, August 20, 2007)

[For more information and instructions about thank-you notes, refer to the author's book, *Networking Nuggets – Connecting For Success*, chapter 12, "A Thank-You Note Is Powerful."]

ADDITIONAL WISDOM
FOR THE SECOND COMMANDMENT

NEVER UNDERESTIMATE THE
APPLAUSE OF ONE

"Have a heart that never hardens, a temper that never tries, and a touch that never hurts."
Charles Dickens, *writer*

"Success has nothing to do with what you gain in life or accomplish for yourself. It's what you do for others."
Danny Thomas, *comedian*

"It is a fine thing to have ability, but the ability to discover ability in others is the true test."
Lou Holtz, *coach, motivational speaker*

"Encourage those who are timid. Take tender care of those who are weak. Be patient with everyone."
Paul, *1 Thessalonians 5:14*

"The best way to knock the chip off someone's shoulder is to pat him on the back."
Author unknown

A QUIZ ABOUT GREATNESS

1. *Name the 5 wealthiest people in the world.*
2. *Name the last 5 Heisman Trophy winners.*
3. *Name the last 5 winners of Miss America.*
4. *Name 5 who have won the Nobel or Pulitzer Prize.*
5. *Name the last 5 Academy Award winning actresses.*
6. *Name the last 5 World Series winners.*

(If you don't do well, don't be embarrassed!)

See how you do on this quiz!

- *List 5 teachers who aided your journey through school.*
- *List 5 people who made you feel appreciated and special.*
- *List 5 people you enjoy spending time with.*
- *List 5 people who helped you through a difficult time.*
- *List 5 people who taught you something that blessed your life.*

THE LESSON:

The people who make a difference in your life are not the "famous", but the ones who care. As the saying goes, *"People don't care how much you know until they know how much you care."*

Ten Commandments of Leadership Networking

A LEADER'S SECOND COMMANDMENT

"Never Underestimate The Applause of One!"

1. **Understand the importance of developing close relationships!**
   - *There is a longing in all of us to be liked, appreciated and valued.*
   - *The biggest challenge for us is dealing effectively with people.*

2. **Lasting relationships develop as we learn the skills and form the habits of:**
   - *Expressing genuine interest in others and their concerns!*
   - *Expressing appreciation for them and their accomplishments!*
   - *Encouraging them in their pursuits!*
   - *Enthusiastically helping them discover their importance!*

3. **"THE APPLAUSE OF ONE" calls <u>YOU</u> to be liberal with praise as you -**
   - *Train your mind to search for the good you can applaud in others.*
   - *Learn to express praise when it is or is not expected.*
     - ➢ *It has the power to draw out the best in others, like polishing silver.*
     - ➢ *"The deepest principle in human nature is the craving to be appreciated." (Wm. James, Harvard University)*

> ➢ *It deposits a great sum in your "credibility" account with the individual.*
> ➢ *It inspires and fires emotional energy.*
> ➢ *It takes what is excellent in others and gives you ownership with them.*
> ➢ *It increases their value and yours.*
> ➢ *It motivates others to do a better job and feel good about themselves and you.*

AN AUDIENCE OF ONE "CLAPPING" – *"Never underestimate it"* BECAUSE:

> ➢ *It's contagious!*
> ➢ *It gives others permission!*
> ➢ *It expresses non-verbal feelings, support and appreciation!*
> ➢ *It sets the right example!*
> ➢ *It reaches the heart of the one you're applauding and all others who support him/her!*

BE LIBERAL WITH PRAISE!

A one word summary for this commandment:

"SUPPORT"

COMMANDMENT #3

Expect Change
And Be Flexible.

VERSATILITY

A LEADER'S
THIRD COMMANDMENT

"Expect Change, And Be Flexible"

After WWII, a young ambitious veteran was sure he could sell vacuum cleaners to the housewives of America. He was trained by a sharp sales manager and with great confidence and enthusiasm drove off to an untapped isolated rural area for his first sales call.

He made his presentation just as he had been trained. After introducing himself to the farm lady, he took a sizable sack of sand from his coat pocket and dumped it in the center of her floor.

"Now, I want you to see what this vacuum cleaner will do! Where is the nearest electrical outlet?"

The lady sheepishly replied, *"Two miles down the road!"*

COMMANDMENT NUMBER THREE:

"EXPECT CHANGE, AND BE FLEXIBLE!"

Counselor, Joe Hale, consulates with those who must manage unexpected tough changes in their lives with these words:

40

"All of life is change.
Every change involves loss
And every loss must be grieved."

Advice columnist, Ann Landers, said, *"If I were asked to give the single most useful bit of advice for all humanity, it would be this: EXPECT TROUBLE AS AN INEVITABLE PART OF LIFE. And when it comes, hold your head high, look it squarely in the eye and say, 'I am bigger than you. You cannot defeat me.'"*

"EXPECT CHANGE"

Everything changes! Nothing stays exactly the same! Change is inevitable, and we should expect it. We should not be ruled by a morbid fear of change, but we should cultivate a mature respect that takes the shocking debilitation out of it.

When my wife, Verlen, and I take a young engaged couple through premarital sessions, one of our goals is to help them discover any unknowns and remove as many surprises as possible. This will help them to expect changes and prepare for needed adjustments.

Joe Hale says, *"All of life is change."* We have no choice but to deal with it!

Yes, but how?

"BE FLEXIBLE"

According to *The Manager Institute*, FLEXIBILITY is the most important single quality one can develop to survive and thrive in "these changing times."

Flexibility requires openness, receptivity and willingness to try new methods, alternatives and techniques. This usually calls for getting our ego out of the way and detaching "self" from the situation to focus more on WHAT'S RIGHT rather than WHO'S RIGHT.

Flexibility leaves room to answer the hard question, as Dr. Phil would say, *"How's that working for you?"* Does it work?

Flexibility is an attitude and mind set that helps you adjust during change and bring forth a positive result in the middle of a negative environment.

NOT PARALYZING FEAR,

BUT PREPARATION TO HANDLE CHANGE

*CHANGE IS INEVITABLE, GROWTH IS OPTIONAL,
I CAST THE DECIDING VOTE!*

The third commandment is vital to successful leadership, networking and selling because:

1) If you don't have a flexible mind set that can accept change, you will be   distracted and defeated when your plans are forced to take a detour.

2) If you can't adjust to change you will become unfocused and be much less effective.

3) If you have a flexibility that *"rolls with the punches"* you can ---

> ➤ Bounce back! General George Patton said, *Success is not how far you fall, but how high you bounce when you hit bottom."*

> ➤ Demonstrate resiliency and elasticity!

> ➤ Show maturity, dependability and good judgment!

> ➤ Exhibit self-control!

A few years ago when the city of Farmers Branch was beginning *Branch Crossing* in our suburb of North Dallas, the first upscale new home had been completed. Civic and business leaders, major real estate personalities and elected officials were invited to the open house ribbon cutting. It was shoulder to shoulder, wall to wall, people. When it came time for Ebby Halliday, the first lady of real estate in Dallas, to speak, she could scarcely be seen, much less be heard. Ebby, a dear friend, stands hardly five feet tall. No one could see her! Also, remember she is over ninety years young, but if you know Ebby, you know her CREATIVE FLEXIBILITY.

As the crowd was called to order and Ebby was introduced, she took hold of the stair way banister and slowly backed up the stair case about three steps as she began a most positive declaration. She made the stairs her speaker's platform. Everyone could see and hear Ebby. She turned an unforeseen challenge into an asset!

She is a superb example of the potential power of the third commandment, *"Expect Change and be Flexible"!*

"Arrange whatever pieces come your way."
Virginia, Woolf, *writer*

YOU MUST DEAL WITH CONTRADICTIONS!

Beliefs and ways of doing things come in two flavors, *"yours"* and *"theirs"*. Like two politicians who unsuccessfully argued a difference until one of them finally said, *"Let's just agree to disagree! You do it your way, and I'll do it the right way!"*

Business and networking will always bring our beliefs and methods into contact with other's beliefs and methods. This will require having enough flexibility to deal constantly with differences as consistently as possible.

The secret is to hold your beliefs while respecting those of others with an openness to understand and learn. Leadership networking requires being a life long student in learning how to face differences and challenges. The rewards will always outweigh the adjustments.

"The rock that is an obstacle in the path of one,
becomes a stepping stone in the path of another."
(unknown)

In the light of the third commandment,
WHAT MAKES HEROES?

I have had the honor this past six months of presiding at
the memorial services of five different veterans of
WWII. Each served America heroically and was
discharged with honors. J.C. Meason had received
three bronze stars for his WWII service at Omaha
Beach and the Battle of the Bulge.

Wars, emergencies, rescues, dilemmas, terrorists
attacks (9/11) ... Changes, sometimes threatening
changes... these make heroes. It happens when
someone handles "change" with courage and strength.

That's what our third commandment is about!

Our one word definition for this commandment is
"VERSATILITY". It's the ability to turn another
direction easily, thus being moveable and adaptable.

ADDITIONAL WISDOM
FOR THE THIRD COMMANDMENT

EXPECT CHANGE
AND BE FLEXIBLE

"Flexibility in a time of great change is a vital quality of leadership."
Brian Tracy, *motivational speaker*

"Change is not made without inconvenience, even from worse to better."
Richard Hooker, *theologian*

"In soloing, as in other activities, it is far easier to start something than to finish it.
Amelia Earhart, *aviator*
(Amelia Earhart embarked on a 19-hour flight from Los Angles to Newark, N.J., making her the first woman to fly solo nonstop from coast to coast, August 24, 1932.)

"I can't believe that God put us on this earth to be ordinary. You might not be able to out-think, out-market, or out-spend your competition, but you can out-work them. No one has ever drowned in sweat."
Lou Holtz, *coach, motivational speaker*

"It has become appallingly obvious that our technology has exceeded our humanity."
Albert Einstein, *physicist*

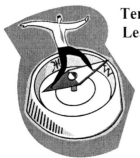

Ten Commandments of Leadership Networking

Commandment #3

"Expect Change, And Be Flexible"

"If I were asked to give what I consider the single most useful bit of advice for all humanity, it would be this: Expect TROUBLE as an inevitable part of life. *And when it comes, hold your head high, look it squarely in the eye and say, 'I am bigger than you. You cannot defeat me.'"*

(*Ann Landers*, Advice Columnist)

1. *"EXPECT CHANGE"* – Everything changes! It is inevitable! We should expect it! We have no choice but to deal with it!

2. *"BE FLEXIBLE"* – It's an attitude and mind set that helps us adjust during change, and energizes us for positive results in the midst of a negative environment.

3. *CHANGE* is inevitable, *GROWTH* is optional, we cast the deciding vote!

4. *COMMANDMENT #3* is vital to success in networking and selling because:

   ➢ It will keep us from being DISTRACTED and DEFEATED!

   ➢ It will help us stay focused and be more effective!

   ➢ With flexibility we can *"roll with the punches"* and:

48

- **Bounce Back**
- **Demonstrate Resiliency and Elasticity**
- **Show Maturity, Dependability and Good Judgment**
- **Keep Control**

5. *LIFE* **demands that we deal with** *CONTRADICTIONS*!

> **Beliefs and methods of doing things come in two flavors, *YOURS* and *THEIRS*.**

> **Networking and selling brings our beliefs/methods into contrast with those of others, day after day. We must have flexibility enough to deal constantly with differences as consistently as possible.**

> **We must be life-long learners in facing differences and changes. The rewards outweigh the adjustments.**

QUESTION:

In the light of Commandment #3, WHAT MAKES HEROES?

Our one word definition for this commandment is *"VERSATILITY"*. It's the ability to turn another direction easily, thus being moveable and adaptable.

COMMANDMENT #4

TRUST is the Foundation.

CHARACTER

THE FOURTH COMMANDMENT

TRUST
IS THE FOUNDATION

Every architect knows that the most vital part of any structure is its foundation. If the foundation is

adequate, something of significance can be built on it, but if it isn't, everything built on that foundation is at risk.

I reference the *Leaning Tower of Pisa*, the bell tower in Pisa, Italy, which leans more than seventeen feet from the perpendicular. While it is a tourist attraction, that was not the builders original goal!

THE FOUNDATION NECESSARY TO BUILD ROCK SOLID RELATIONSHIPS IS *TRUST*!

The most important ingredient is <u>ANY</u> relationship is *<u>TRUST</u>*!

Every business deal proceeds from that base. If that basis fails, no productive relationship will develop.
KNOW, LIKE, TRUST

Generally speaking we do business with those we *know,* *like* and *trust.* Each of these items is vital to a successful business transaction, but *trust* is by far the most important. For example, I may invite you to fly from Dallas to Houston with me. You *know* me and you *like* me, but when you discover that I will be piloting the plane, you will have second thoughts about going. You can't trust me to fly an airplane. I am not a pilot, therefore, you could not possibly trust me to get us there safely. You *know* me. You *like* me. But when it comes to piloting an airplane you have no grounds (foundation) to *trust* me.

THE FOUNDATION OF TRUST
MUST BE THE LAID

Since *"ENRON,"* and numerous other betrayals of trust in every section of our world, we must concern ourselves with carefully protecting everything about us that speaks of our integrity. People are more and more aware that they must be wary. We must be reminded that effective leadership and networking reaches beyond meeting and talking with prospective clients to intentionally establishing solid confidence. Solid confidence is built on the firm ground of trust. Two things that you need to intentionally seek to establish in your followers and potential clients are:

➢ Confidence in your ability and your willingness to meet their needs.

➢ Your reliability in following through with commitments to them.

WHAT IS TRUST?

The word *"trust"* literally means *firmness*. My dad used to say of a trustworthy man, *"He has timber in him!"* That meant, he had strength; was solid and dependable. But also notice that the expression denotes the usefulness of the person. A person with *"timber"* in him will get the job, or get my business, or get my following, because of the likely good the *"timber"* in him will mean to me. I will choose to put my weight down on him because of a certain trust factor. The basic word from which we get the English word *"trust"* is the root word *"true"*.

To get a mental picture of *"trust"* we need to explore the <u>*Thesaurus*</u> and create a list of synonyms that bring to life this greatest of all foundation virtues.

➢ In "the market place," *"trust"* is:

* Honesty

* Integrity

* Reliability

* Justice

➢ In an individual, *"trust"* is evidenced when one is:

* Reliable

* Dependable

* Faithful

* Responsible

* Credible

SOLVE THIS MYSTERY

In some of the most notorious criminal cases, why do defense attorneys often have their male clients appear in court dressed in a dark blue suit, white shirt, maroon tie and their hair freshly trimmed and faces neatly shaven?

The answer is simple, and very important! A smart attorney knows that appearance has everything to do with CREDIBILITY. *"Man looks on the outward appearance ..."(1 Samuel 16:7)*. Only God can see the heart! Humans can only see *"the outward appearance"*.

John T. Molloy, years ago (1988), made an extensive study in his book, <u>*Dress For Success*</u>, about who Americans are most likely to trust. His conclusions agree completely with ... the dark blue suit, white shirt, maroon tie and neat grooming.

WE MUST LOOK, TALK AND ACT
LIKE WE CAN BE TRUSTED!

In this issue of *trust* we are responsible for creating our own believability and credibility. *Trust* comes as a result of at least five things:

1) Do I *think* like I can be trusted?

2) Do I *look* like I can be trusted?

3) Do I *talk* like I can be trusted?

4) Do I *act* like I can be trusted?

5) Do *my associates* give others the feeling I can be trusted?

DAVE VS JOE

A few years ago a very damaging hail storm hit the older housing addition where our home is located. Almost every roof had to be replaced. Roofing salesmen invaded this rather conservative neighborhood with their sales pitches. Dave met me in our church parking lot, just four blocks from our house, with a handful of his business cards, dressed in a tank top shirt, shorts, sandals, shaved head and a large beaded necklace. He wanted my endorsement to sell this older, conservative neighborhood roofing. He didn't sell a single roof … not because Dave is a crooked, fly-by-night salesman, but because he looked like he was!

On the other hand, Joe, driving a white Ford pickup, dressed in nice neat conservative business casual attire

… looked, talked and acted like he was professional and could be trusted … sold more roofs than all the other salesmen combined. Yes, he first sold the most influential people in the addition, and their confidence in Joe gave him leverage (trust deposits) to sell other home owners.

REAL GENUINE *"TRUST"*
IS <u>CHARACTER</u>!

Trust is about being real and worthy of confidence. As we live it, we earn it by <u>who </u>we are! Nothing is more essential to success! *Trust* is the foundation!

The one word synonym for *"TRUST"* is:
"CHARACTER".

ADDITIONAL WISDOM
FOR THE FOURTH COMMANDMENT

TRUST IS THE FOUNDATION

"Success is more permanent when you achieve it without destroying your principles."
Walter Cronkite, *TV news anchor*

"Character is like a tree, and reputation is like a shadow. The shadow is what we think of it; the tree is the real thing."
Abraham Lincoln, *16th U.S. president*

"The supreme quality for leadership is unquestionably integrity. Without it, no real success is possible."
"A people that values its privileges above its principles soon loses both."
Dwight Eisenhower, *34th U.S. president*

"To be trusted is a greater compliment than to be loved."
George MacDonald, *author*

"God hasn't called me to be successful. He's called me to be faithful."
Mother Teresa, *Catholic nun*

"Goldwynisms" – Samuel Goldwyn was a movie mogul known for statements that sound a lot like Yogi Berra. They were known as *"Goldwnyisms"* and here are a few:

- ➤ *"They stayed away in droves."*
- ➤ *"Any man who goes to a psychologist should have his head examined."*
- ➤ *"Don't pay attention to the critics; don't even ignore them."*
- ➤ *"Never make forecasts, especially about the future."*
- ➤ *"I don't think anyone should write his autobiography until after he's dead."*
- ➤ *"Give me a smart idiot over a stupid genius any day."*
- ➤ (Honesty) *"I don't want yes-men around me. I want everyone to tell the truth, even if it costs them their jobs."*

Saturday Evening Post, *March/April, 2007, p.18*

The Fourth Commandment

TRUST
IS THE FOUNDATION

1. The most important ingredient in _____ relationship is _____ !

2. The foundation of trust must be laid!

> **What is trust? How do you define it?**

In the market place trust is:

_____

In an individual trust is evidenced when one is:

_____

3. Solve this mystery:
   Why do attorneys often have their male clients appear in court dressed in a dark blue suit, white shirt and maroon tie, with their hair freshly trimmed and faces neatly shaven?

> **C_____**

> **We must *look*, *talk* and *act* like we can be trusted! (In that order)**

> ➤ **Trust comes as a result of at least five things:**

1) Do I _____ like I can be trusted?

2) Do I _____ like I can be trusted?

3) Do I _____ like I can be trusted?

4) Do I _____ like I can be trusted?

5) Do ___ _____ give others the feeling I can be trusted?

4. Real genuine trust is C_____ !

The author, George MacDonald, has said, *"To be trusted is a greater compliment than to be loved."* This is true because love has its foundation in trust!

COMMANDMENT #5

Wherever You Are, Be All There!

FOCUS

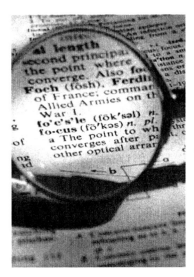

A LEADER'S
FIFTH COMMANDMENT

Wherever You Are, Be All There!

*"In basketball – as in life –
true joy comes from being fully present
in each and every moment."*

Phil Jackson, *NBA coach*

In the early 1950's missionary to the Incas of South America, Jim Elliot, wrote this proverbial saying, *"Wherever you are, be all there!"* A recent well-received movie, *The Point of the Spear*, documents the depths of commitment he and his fellow missionaries had. It also depicts the ultimate fruits of total focus.

This fifth commandment is at the very center of the *Ten Commandments of Leadership Networking*, WHY? The center of anything is what tends to hold it together. Leadership demands the ability to center on something, to prioritize.

In the Bible, there is a parable about *inattention* which has a soldier who has failed at his assignment to keep guard over a captured enemy confessing to his superior, *"While I was busy doing something else, the prisoner disappeared!"* (1 Kings 20:35-43) Too often, when we have failed at a very important business responsibility, it is because we were busy doing something else and the business opportunity disappeared.

THIS COMMANDMENT REQUIRES *FOCUS*!

James, the New Testament writer, says, *"A double minded man is unstable in all his ways."* (James 1:8) A *"double minded man"* has a divided mind. He is irresolute, uncertain, half-hearted and suffers from having *"two minds"*.

There is an old saying about such an unfocused mind --- *"He got on his horse and rode off in all four directions!"*

Focus requires us to fix and settle our minds on one thing! It is undivided attention and full concentration.

How can the professional golfers perform so well in the midst of a multitude of spectators? FOCUS!

The great Apostle Paul, who wrote a good number of letters from a Roman prison cell stated it this way, *"...This one thing I do; forgetting what is behind and straining toward what is ahead ..."* (Philippians 3:13).

IT DEMANDS EFFORT!

This commandment requires the mental, emotional and physical energy of:

> *ALERTNESS* – Active vigilance and brisk watchfulness, the opposite of mental laziness, a form of being *"psyched up"*.

> *DESIRE* – Passion for and wanting desperately to achieve and *"win"*.

"LOSERS"

Often losers are present in body only and are usually viewed as *"absent minded"* and are given to mental errors. They are:

> *NOT THERE*

> *NOT "WITH US"*

> *NOT A TEAM PLAYER*

> *INDIFFERENT TO THE BUSINESS, THE PRODUCT, THE GOALS*

> *UNCARING OF THEIR RESPONSIBILITIES*

 *"WHEREVER YOU ARE, BE ALL THERE"* relates to a sense of LOYALTY. I am an American! I live in Farmers Branch, Texas! It is the place of my home, my school district, my church and my business. I pledge allegiance to these. It is my duty! I am bound to be trustworthy, reliable and responsible to these! This is where I am! I must be "ALL THERE!"

HOW CAN ONE BE "ALL THERE"?

1) Exert the energy intentionally! Fly the flag! Wear the T-shirt!

2) Remember, almost nothing happens automatically! Freedom is not free, and "there ain't no free lunch!"

3) Accept your responsibility for *"being there"*, no substitutes accepted.

4) Discipline yourself to *"pay attention"*! Inattention and indecision are fatal twins!

5) Acknowledge and accept that thinking, learning and participating are hard work!

6) Test yourself by asking, *"How badly do I want it?"*

# SUCCESS

KEY MOTIVATORS:

As you practice the fifth commandment here are five keys that will unlock your own mind and the hearts of those with whom you do business.

1) *You are your company's best ad!* Other items may be helpful, but you are the most important advertisement for your organization or product.

2) *Your business card is your second chance for a good first impression.* They will see you first and then hear your voice, and hopefully these will be powerfully impressive, but make sure your business card makes up any thing that might be lacking. Your business card is the most inexpensive and the most important piece of literature you give out.

3) *Nobody is good at everything!* Know your gifts and your field of endeavor and be "all there" where you are the best.

4) *Their name is the most important thing you say!* You must be "all there" and listen for and remember their names. This will far outweigh anything else you say.

5) *"Money talks, but CHOCOLATE sings!"* Come bearing gifts! The wisest and richest man who ever lived said, *"A gift opens the way for the giver and ushers him into the presence of the great."* (Solomon, Proverbs 18:16)

"WHEREVER YOU ARE, BE ALL THERE!"

Our synonym for the fifth commandment is *"FOCUS"*.

If you avoid distraction and stay focused, you will capitalize on the potential of every moment and every activity you are engaged in, benefiting yourself, your business, and the people you lead or serve or want to do more business with.

*ADDITIONAL WISDOM
FOR THE FIFTH
COMMANDMENT*

**WHEREVER YOU ARE,
BE ALL THERE**

"A person always doing his or her best becomes a natural leader, just by example."
> Joe DiMaggio, *baseball player*

"When you're riding, only the race in which you're riding is important."
> Bill Shoemaker, *jockey*

"Your own resolution to succeed is more important than any other one thing."
> Abraham Lincoln, *16ᵗʰ U.S. President*

"It's faith in something and enthusiasm for something that makes life worth living."
Oliver Wendell Holmes, Sr., *physician*

"I have discovered in life that there are ways of getting almost anywhere you want to go – if you really want to go."
Langston Hughes, *writer*

"If a man has done his best, what else is there?"
George Patton, *general*

"Do what you can, with what you have, where you are."
Theodore Roosevelt, *26ᵗʰ U.S. president*

"Concentrate all your thoughts upon the work at hand. The sun's rays do not burn until brought to a focus."
Alexander Graham Bell, *inventor*

"It's no accident that things are more likely to go your way when you stop worrying about whether you're going to win or lose, and focus your full attention on what's happening right at this moment."
Phil Jackson, *basketball coach*

"Aerodynamically, the bumblebee shouldn't be able to fly, but the bumblebee doesn't know it so it goes on flying anyway."

Mary Kay Ash, *entrepreneur*

"It is always self-defeating to pretend to be the style of a generation younger than your own. It simply erases your own experience in history."

Renata Alder, *writer*

**A LEADER'S
FIFTH COMMANDMENT:**

Wherever You Are,
Be All There!

This commandment requires _____!

Focus requires us to fix and settle our minds on one thing! It is undivided attention and full concentration.

This commandment requires the mental, emotional and physical energy of:

➤ _____ – Active vigilance and brisk watchfulness, the opposite of mental laziness, a form of being *"psyched up"*.

➤ _____ – Passion for and wanting desperately to achieve and *"win"*.

HOW CAN ONE BE "ALL THERE"?

1) Exert the energy intentionally! Fly the flag! Wear the T-shirt!

2) Remember, almost nothing happens automatically! Freedom is not free, and "there ain't no free lunch!"

3) Accept your responsibility for *"being there"*, no substitutes accepted.

4) Discipline yourself to *"pay attention"*! Inattention and indecision are fatal twins!

5) Acknowledge and accept that thinking, learning and participating are hard work!

6) Test yourself by asking, *"How badly do I want it?"*

KEY MOTIVATORS:

As you practice the fifth commandment here are five keys that will unlock your own mind and the hearts of those with whom you do business.

1) _____ *are your company's best ad!*

2) *Your* _____ _____ *is your second chance for a good first impression.*

3) *Nobody is good at* _____!

4) _____ _____ *is the most important thing you say!*

5) *"Money talks, but* _____ *sings!"*

Our synonym for the fifth commandment is
"FOCUS".

73

COMMANDMENT #6

People are usually down on,
what they are not
up on.

COMMUNICATE

A LEADER'S SIXTH COMMANDMENT:

PEOPLE ARE USUALLY <u>DOWN</u> ON

WHAT THEY ARE NOT <u>UP</u> ON!

What continues to be one of our biggest and never-ending challenges in this time, which has been called *"The Communication Age"*, is COMMUNICATION!

SEVEN REASONS WHY <u>COMMUNICATION</u> IS VITAL TO YOUR SUCCESS:

1) People naturally resist change when they don't participate in the decision making process.

2) Everyone wants to take pride in their organization and take ownership in being associated with the company or product at some decision making level.

3) Everyone has an ego which is to be considered before making a decision that involves them.

4) When you communicate with any individual you help raise their level of self esteem.

5) If you want the full support of people, involve them in some *action process*, and the sooner, the better.

6) People will support what they help create. The more they participate in a new project, the more they will

support it. Conversely, the more they feel excluded, the more they will resist.

7) People feel slighted and manipulated when they have no input, or are not consulted. If you have *problem people,* let them share in the solution by asking them, *"What do you think?",* or *"What do you want?"*

THE *"SPOUSE TEST"* PROVES THE SIXTH COMMANDMENT

When your spouse hears of something you failed to tell them about, isn't it always a *"downer"*? But the same is also true with your boss or business associate. This proves that we all must *"Major in Communication"* in the continuing education of life.

But, what does it take to communicate?

A *"CHECK LIST"*
TO HELP YOU COMMUNICATE:

1) TOOLS:
   You must have items with which to communicate, such as ---

   ➢ *Business Cards* with complete contact information.

   ➢ *Name Tag(s)* appropriate to the occasion.

   ➢ *Technology* that includes phones, computers, electronic messaging.

   ➢ *Printed Materials* ... letterheads, envelops, cards, brochures.

[Remember, in communication, *"one size does <u>not</u> fit all"*! It has been proven that in reaching some clients as many as seven different ways of communication were needed before finally getting the message to them. Always be mindful of the age and the *"electronic availability"* of your prospect. Some people are insulted and threatened when only electronic communication is offered.]

2) SKILLS:
   Know how, includes using an electronic medium of communication and being there *"live and in person"*. We can learn to be good at both, but the most challenging is communicating effectively when meeting others *face to face*. Here are some simple guidelines every networker must know!

   ➢ Always have your business cards with you!

   ➢ Always have your business cards where you can reach them with your left hand while shaking hands with your right hand. (I always keep my business cards in my left coat pocket, and place the business cards I receive from others in my shirt pocket.)

   ➢ Always wear your name tag on your right lapel so that as you meet others they can clearly read your name.

   ➢ Always smile, have a welcoming voice tone and professional body language.

[Remember you are a *"Communication Major"*! You are a life long learner in this vital field! Read the books, attend the training, hear the seminars and workshops on CDs in your car. It will pay great dividends!]

COMMUNICATION QUIZ

True or False?

   1) The more *I* talk, and the more *they* listen the more they will like me and trust me.

True or False?

   2) The more *they* talk, and the more *I* listen, the more they will like me and trust me.

True or False?

   3) People don't feel a part until they get to talk.

True or False?

   4) Counselors and psychotherapists have found that *active listening* creates trust.

True or False?

   5) Always include your business card in everything you mail out.

[Answers: (1) F; (2) T; (3) T; (4) T; (5) T]

79

LEADERSHIP AND COMMUNICATION

Leadership carries with it the responsibility of clear communication. It has been said, *"Leadership is INFLUENCE!"* How does one have influence?

Here's the formula:

Leadership (influence) = *Credibility* + *Communication*

* *Credibility* is who you are!
* *Communication* is what you say and how you say it!

This formula suggests that communication is fifty percent of leadership. While credibility (trust) is extremely vital, the absence of effective communication severely limits leadership... probably cuts it in half!

In leadership the bottom line is to make sure you *tell people what you want them to do* and *give them permission to do it.*

All of us are vulnerable to making the assumption that others are "on the same page" with us, that they know what we are thinking, and that they are in tune with it. However, that easily-made assumption is commonly not the case. And that is almost always counterproductive to one's leadership and networking.

Our one word synonym for the sixth commandment, *"PEOPLE ARE USUALLY <u>DOWN</u> ON WHAT THEY ARE NOT <u>UP</u> ON!"* is:

"COMMUNICATE!"

ADDITIONAL WISDOM
FOR THE SIXTH
COMMANDMENT

PEOPLE ARE USUALLY DOWN ON
WHAT THEY ARE NOT UP ON

"We're all Christ and we're all Hitler. We want Christ to win. What would He have done if He had advertisements, TV, records, films and newspapers? The miracle today is communication. So let's use it."
John Lennon, *singer – entertainer*

"If people are having trouble communicating, the least they could do is shut up about it."
Tom Lehrer, *comedian*

"I never thought it was my style or the words I used that made a difference: It was the content. I wasn't a great communicator; I communicated great things."
Ronald Reagan, *40th U.S. president*

"Make a habit of dominating the listening and let the customer dominate the talking."
Brian Tracy, *motivational speaker*

"Feeling gratitude and not expressing it is like wrapping a present and not giving it."

William Arthur Ward, *scholar*

A LEADER'S SIXTH COMMANDMENT

PEOPLE ARE USUALLY <u>DOWN</u> ON

WHAT THEY ARE NOT <u>UP</u> ON!

While we live in *"The Communication Age"*, one of our never ending challenges is COMMUNICATION!

7 REASONS WHY COMMUNICATION IS VITAL TO YOUR SUCCESS

1) *People naturally resist change when they don't participate in the decision making process.*

2) *Everyone wants to take pride in their organization and take ownership in being associated with the company or product at some decision making level.*

3) *Everyone has an ego which is to be considered before making a decision that involves them.*

4) *When you communicate with any individual you help raise their level of self esteem.*

5) *If you want the full support of people, involve them in some <u>action</u>, and the sooner, the better.*

6) *People will support what they help create. The more they participate in a new project, the more they will support it. Conversely, the more they feel excluded, the more they will resist.*

7) *People feel slighted and manipulated when they have no input, or are not consulted. If you have "problem people", let them share in the solution by asking them, "What do you think?" or "What do you want?"*

THE *"SPOUSE TEST"* PROVES
THE 6TH COMMANDMENT!

When your spouse hears of something you failed to tell him/her about, isn't it always a *"downer"*? But the same is also true with your boss or business associate. This proves that we must all MAJOR IN COMMUNICATION.

A *"CHECK LIST"* TO
HELP YOU COMMUNICATE

1) TOOLS: *Business Cards; Name Tag(s); Technology; Printed Materials…..*
2) SKILLS: *Keeps tools available; Wear a smile; Speak with grace; Have professional body language.*

COMMUNICATION QUIZ
True or False?

1) The more *I* talk, and the more *they* listen, the more they will like me and trust me.

2) The more *they* talk, and the more *I* listen, the more they will like me and trust me.

3) People don't feel a part until they get to talk.

4) Counselors and psychotherapists have found that *active listening* creates trust.

5) Always include your business card in everything you mail out.

THE LEADERSHIP AND COMMUNICATION
FORMULA

Credibility + Communication = Leadership (influence)
- *Credibility* is who you are!
- *Communication* is what you say and how you say it!

The synonym for the 6th Commandment, "PEOPLE ARE USUALLY *DOWN* ON WHAT THEY ARE NOT *UP* ON!" is *COMMUNICATE.*

COMMANDMENT

Timing is Everything.

FLOW

A LEADER'S
SEVENTH COMMANDMENT:

TIMING
IS
EVERYTHING!

Solomon said, *"There is a time for everything, and a season for every activity under heaven: a time to be born and a time to die, a time to plant and a time to uproot, a time to kill and a time to heal, a time to tear down and a time to build, a time to weep and a time to laugh, a time to mourn and a time to dance ..."* (Ecclesiastes 3:1-8)

In the whole list, the wisest and richest man who ever lived named fourteen opposites to illustrate a point. Our pursuits are good in their proper time, but unprofitable when pursued at the wrong time.

THE LAW OF TIMING

Does *"the law of timing"* really exist? If so, can it be proven? Yes, it is as much a law as *"the law of gravity"*, and just as provable!

1) Does timing matter to the farmer? Almost all of farming is based on the time and season of the year. Crops are planted in the spring, cultivated in the summer and harvested in the fall. Violate that timing and a crop failure is sure.

2) Every area of life, profession and skill is affected by timing! Think about these:

> Ranching
> Hunting
> Fishing
> Cooking
> Gardening
> Building
> Sports
    * Golfing
    * Baseball
    * Football, etc

3) No part of our lives is exempt from the importance of timing, especially in the realm of leadership, networking and business. Consider the power of appropriate timing in:

> Sales calls
> Closing the sale
> Advertising and announcements
> Affirming and supporting others

THE _RESULTS_ YOU GET IN ANYTHING USUALLY HAS A GREAT DEAL TO DO WITH _TIMING_!

When Bob Hope, one of the most successful entertainers of all time, was asked to lecture to the drama department of a major university, he said, *"You can teach them everything but timing!"*

Looking back on the spectacular careers of performers like Hope, Jack Benny, George Burns and Lucille Ball, you realize that at the top of all their giftedness was a flawless sense of timing. They could take the most simple thing and make it hilariously funny with just a well timed pause, facial expression or gesture.

The secret of effective leadership and networking is much the same. It is thinking, saying and doing the right thing at the right time!

IN LIFE _WHEN_ IS AS IMPORTANT AS _WHAT_ OR _WHERE_ !

The Latin expression *"Carpe Diem"* literally means, *"seize the day"*. It's about timing! Prompting us to make the most of opportunities while the door is open and coaching one to *"strike while the iron is hot"*. The Bible puts it: *"Make the most of every opportunity"* (Ephesians 5:16).

We must be alert to *times of receptivity*, when there is an openness ... major times like Solomon mentions ... *"Born, Die, Plant, Uproot, Kill, Heal, Tear Down, Build Up, Weep, Laugh, Mourn, Dance, Be Silent, Speak ..."* Occasions when timing is everything!

THE MAGIC OF
TIMELY FOLLOW UP

If you follow-up business in a timely manner with your clients, it will have a marvelous effect in the way they see you.

Your timing will cause them to see you as:

- <u>Professional</u> – (you mean business)

- <u>Dependable</u> – (you do what you say)

- <u>Responsible</u> – (you are awake, aware and alive to others)

- <u>Organized</u> – (you know when and where it's at)

- <u>Courteous</u> – (you have good business manners and etiquette)

- <u>Thoughtful</u> – (you are unselfish and mindful of others)

FLOW

A synonym that summarizes the Seventh Commandment, *"Timing Is Everything,"* is the word *FLOW*– like the right beat or timing in a piece of great music... Bringing the right notes and words together at the right time.

The best music is made by the cooperation and coordination of several musicians playing together to produce a symphony of complimentary and harmonious offerings.

Our business and community pursuits are much the same. Progress and productivity that is the most beautiful and helpful requires the attentive cooperation and coordination of a number of players. Competent leaders and networkers are needed. Players that have developed good judgment in regard to timing and proper management of the flow of coordinating efforts will make progress possible. That good judgment may reside in leaders out of sheer giftedness, or more likely, through experience at networking and learning from others. At any rate, every business and community enterprise needs the blessing and benefits that timeliness–the smooth flow of words and actions–can bring.

THE CLOCK OF LIFE

The clock of life is wound but once,
And no man has the power to tell
Just when the hands will stop,
At late or early hour.

Now is the only time you own,
Live, love, toil with a will.
Place no faith in tomorrow,
For the hands may then stand still.

In the September 3, 2007, issue of *Fortune* magazine, page 26, Kip Tindell, CEO and Co-Chairman of the Container Store, puts an interesting twist on modeling when he says: *"Someone made me a bumper sticker that reads "GOT WAKE?", and I keep it with me all the time.*

I have a theory that your wake, just like a boat's, is much bigger than you realize. Everything we do – and what we don't do --- impacts the people around you a lot more than you think."

ADDITIONAL WISDOM
FOR THE
SEVENTH COMMANDMENT

TIMING IS EVERYTHING

"Time is the most valuable thing man can spend."
Diogenes Laertius, *writer*

"They always say that time changes things, but you actually have to change them yourself."
Andy Warhol, *artist*

"Half of our life is spent trying to find something to do with the time we have rushed through life trying to save."
Will Rogers, *humorist*

"You may delay, but time will not."
"Dost thou love life? Then do not squander time, for that is the stuff life is made of."
Benjamin Franklin, *author and statesman*

"Practice the golden rule of management: Manage others the way you would like to be managed."

Brian Tracy, *motivational speaker*

A LEADER'S
SEVENTH COMMANDMENT

TIMING
IS
EVERYTHING!

"There is a time for everything ..."
Solomon, *Ecclesiastes 3:1-8*

1. *"The Law of Timing"*, does it really exist?
   - Does it matter to the farmer?
   - Every area of life is affected by timing!
   - Business is certainly not exempt from appropriate timing.

2. The <u>*results*</u> you get in anything usually has a great deal to do with <u>*timing*</u> !

3. In life, <u>*when*</u> is as important as <u>*what*</u> or <u>*where*</u> !
   - *"Carpe Diem"* – "seize the day".
   - Times of receptivity and openness ... when one has "permission" to act.

4. The magical power of timely follow-up --- because it causes others to see you as:
   - *Professional* – you mean business!
   - *Dependable* – you do what you say you will do!
   - *Responsible* – you are awake, aware and alive for business!

- *Organized* – you know when and where "it's at"!
- *Courteous* – you have good business manners and etiquette!
- *Thoughtful* – you are unselfish and mindful of others!

 A synonym that summarizes the Seventh Commandment, *"Timing Is Everything"*, is the word FLOW ... like the beat or timing in a piece of great music ... bringing the right notes and words together at the right time.

Competent leaders and networkers have developed good judgment in regard to timing and proper management of the flow of coordinating efforts that will make progress possible.

> *"...Time ... is the stuff life is made of."*
> **Benjamin Franklin**

COMMANDMENT #8

People Do...
What People See

MODEL

A LEADER'S EIGHTH COMMANDMENT

PEOPLE DO WHAT PEOPLE SEE!

It has been said that this is the greatest motivational principle of all. Is that an accurate conclusion?

We no doubt live in the most *visual age* in the history of the world. We are a *visual* people. We must be. Think on this list:

> **Graphic Visuals**
>
> - **Road Signs**
> - **Airport Signage**
> - **Computer Keyboards and Symbols**
> - **Elevator Control Panels**
> - **Athletic Symbols in Football, Baseball, Basketball, Tennis, Golf, etc**

…. And the list goes on ….

Often one simple drawing speaks a bunch!

One of the most successful sessions we have at our networking group, *Branch Out*, is *"Show & Tell"*.

Yes, it presents a real challenge for some businesses to come up with a visual that tells the story of their company or product, but the exercise always proves helpful to the presenter as well as to the audience.

John Custer, owner of a company called, *"Banners & Signs, Etc."* always brings a sample of his products to each networking session. It has been so successful that he calls his thirty second commercial of demonstrating his merchandise, *"Show & Sell"*.

Warren Witt, *"the blind guy"*, with Budget Blinds of Dallas, always displays a sample of his most recent window dressing products. With these salesmen it's always more than words, it's *"Show & Tell"*.

WHY IS *"SHOW & TELL"*
SO EFFECTIVE IN CONNECTING?

Zig Ziglar says that connecting with people is:

- **87% Sight** (Appearance, Facial expressions, Body Language)

- **7% Hearing**

- **3.5% Smell**

- **1.5% Touch**

- **1% Taste**

The eighth commandment *"People Do What People See"*, recognizes the most powerful of the five human senses, SIGHT.

While every physical handicap is a sincere concern in America, the visually handicapped receive more federal and state benefits than any other, because sight is so vital to success in almost every area of life … physical sight … but even more so, *mental insight*.

LEADERSHIP DEPENDS ON
WHAT PEOPLE SEE

We must model what we want to see in others! As leaders it is our responsibility to set the example.

> *"Example is not the main thing*
> *in influencing others ...*
> *it is the only thing."*
>
> *(Albert Schweitzer,* 1952 Nobel Peace Prize winner*)*

Most people must see something in order to do it or understand it. To say the least, learning comes much faster when the subject can be made visual. Coaches diagram plays for their athletes, take them through drills, and have them watch films. My high school coach called this "skull practice." He meant exercising the brain ... which was more important than mindless play. That's real coaching!

THE LEVERAGE OF EXAMPLE
MOVES PEOPLE!

There is in every human some resistance to *"orders"*. It is obvious that for leadership to be effective there must be a *"trickle down influence"*. The tough question must be faced ... *Can we persuasively demand of others what we are unwilling to do ourselves?*

Lee Iaccoa put it this way, *"The speed of the boss is the speed of the team."*

MODEL

It has been said, *"Imitation is the sincerest form of flattery!"* Give them something to imitate!

"Model" is a good one word synonym for the leadership commandment, *People Do What People See*, because:

➢ Leaders lead by influence, thus influence is leadership!

➢ Leadership influences others by giving them the pattern you want duplicated!

➢ A picture is still worth more than a thousand words!

➢ It takes a positive model to get a positive response! A negative model gets a negative response!

➢ Successful businesses have found that skits and role play train effective employees!

The lines of an old poem go like this:

"I'd rather see a sermon,
  than hear one any day!
I'd rather one would walk with me,
  than merely point the way!
The eye's a better pupil, more willing than the ear,

Fine counsel is confusing, but examples always clear!"

Jesus taught, *"...let your light shine before men, that they may see your good deeds..."* (Matthew 5:16).

I bet that good advice will bring the right light to any circumstance or enterprise. You can't go wrong leading by example!

 ## *ADDITIONAL WISDOM FOR THE EIGHTH COMMANDMENT*

PEOPLE DO WHAT PEOPLE SEE

"A person always doing his or her best becomes a natural leader, just by example."
Joe DiMaggio, *baseball player*

"Leadership is the art of getting someone else to do something you want done because he wants to do it."
Dwight Eisenhower, *34ᵗʰ U.S. president*

"If your actions inspire others to dream more, learn more, do more and become more, you are a leader."
John Quincy Adams, *6ᵗʰ U.S. president*

"Whenever you do a thing, act as if all the world were watching."
Thomas Jefferson, *3ʳᵈ U.S. president*

A Leader's Eighth Commandment:

PEOPLE *DO* WHAT PEOPLE *SEE*.

It has been said that this is the greatest motivational principle of all.
Is that an accurate conclusion?

1. Why is *"SHOW & TELL" so powerful?*

   ➢ Because most people are *visual*... and even more so now! ("Copy Cats" in behavior, fashions, fades, etc)

   ➢ *Connecting with people* is:

   _____% Sight,   _____% Hearing

   _____% Smell   _____% Touch

   _____% Taste,

   and "body language" really matters!

2. We must *model* what we want to see in others.

   Why?

   ➢ They must usually *see* something in order to *do* it or *understand* it. To say the least, they will learn much *faster*, if they see it done. *(Try "Role Play".)*

   ➢ A picture is *still* worth more than a thousand words.

<u>Group Assignment</u>: (Each one is given a piece of a puzzle, but the picture of the completed puzzle is kept hidden.)

"You are an important piece of the picture. Your assignment is to put your piece in the proper place to complete the picture."

- **What would help you more than anything else to get your piece of the puzzle (picture) in the right place?** (Answer: To <u>see</u> the whole <u>picture</u> of what the completed puzzle looks like.)

- **Albert Schweitzer, 1952 Nobel Peace Prize winner, said, *"Example is not the main thing in influencing others, it is the only thing."***

3. The *leverage* of example moves people!

- **Leaders lead by __(influence)__!**

  __(Influence)__ is leadership!

- **Lee Iaccoa said,**
  "The speed of the boss is the speed of the team."

- **Leadership is accomplished by *"the trickle down effect"*.**

- **Can we effectively demand of others what we are unwilling to do ourselves?**

SYNONYM: *<u>MODEL</u>* – Illustrate what you want others to do! Set a standard to imitate. Show them a pattern to duplicate. BE an example of what you want.

COMMANDMENT #9

Share the Big Picture

VISION

A LEADER'S NINTH COMMANDMENT

"SHARE THE BIG PICTURE"

Dr. Shirley Neely, Secretary of Education for the State of Texas, says,

"Sometimes you have to tell your own story! You're the only one who can!"

A leader must cast the vision and be able to tell the organization's story. *"The Big Picture"* is the overall goal and purpose of your business, your position or your product. It's the *umbrella* that covers the whole thing.

Yes, there are always two sides of the coin! In sharing the broad view or helping others to see the whole picture some say too much and some say too little.

"TOO MUCH"

Remember the little boy who asked his dad a question about *"the birds and the bees"*? His blushing dad said, *"Son, I'm busy!"* The boy asked again, and his father replied, *"Son, I'm just too busy right now! Go ask your mother!"* The boy paused, then said, *"I didn't want to know that much about it."*

"TOO LITTLE"

The late Oliver Wendell Holmes, Jr., U.S. Supreme Court Justice, was riding the train when the Conductor came by to collect tickets. Mr. Holmes couldn't find his ticket. As he searched every pocket and his brief case, the Conductor assured the well known Supreme Court Justice, *"It's alright, we know you and trust you!"* But Mr. Holmes explained, *"I must find that ticket, so I will know where I'm going."*

While these stories are humorous, they teach a needed lesson in leadership. We can share too many details and run others off, or we can be so ill-informed that we cause others to distrust our leadership.

"THE BIG PICTURE"
IS HOW YOU SEE IT— YOUR VISION!

Perhaps the biggest challenge of all is to *"Share the Big Picture"* about your company, organization or product *in one sentence.* A sentence that defines who you are and what you do ... some call it your *"tag line"*. That's what a logo, motto or slogan is about! That's hard, but if you can do it ... it means that you truly have a clear understanding of it. That's leadership!

Keith Martino, a dear friend, formerly worked at an executive level for Fed Ex. He now serves as a business consultant and sales trainer for major corporations through his own company, *The Leadership Institute.* On one occasion in the early 1990's Keith invited me to a luncheon at the Fairmont Hotel in downtown Dallas with the well known football coach, Lou Holtz. Coach Holtz has often served as a consultant for major companies. That day he shared with us how he questions company employees about their understanding of *"The Big Picture"* as it relates to them by asking:

> ➢ *"What do you do for this company?"*

> ➢ *"Who is your customer?"*

> ➢ *"What does the customer want?"*

Their answers to these questions reveal their understanding of the role they play in making the company successful. ... *"The Big Picture"* as they see it!

If you were given one minute on national TV to answer Lou Holtz's questions, what would the multiplied millions hear you say?

THE COMPANY NAME
CAN *"SHARE THE BIG PICTURE"*

Sometimes the company name *"Shares The Big Picture"*, and that is very important. A good friend, Joe Catalano, put in an Italian eating establishment in Farmers Branch (North Dallas) and named it *Amichee's*. Only after he had his sign put up and all the menus and literature printed, did he discover that there was already an Italian restaurant in the adjoining city of Carrollton named *Amichee's*. At great expense the name change had to happen. But what would the new name be? Joe is a member of the Farmers Branch Chamber of Commerce, and some of us in our networking group, *Branch Out,* talked with him about the problem. We reasoned:

> ➢ His name is Joe!
>
> ➢ He is full-blooded Italian and uses some of his mother's delicious recipes!
>
> ➢ He wants to share excellent dinning with patrons!

Why not call it what it is? – *"Joe's Italian Café"!*

Now over five years later, *Joe's Italian Cafe* continues to grow! The name defines his goal and purpose. It *"Shares The Big Picture".*

Jeff Crilley, Emmy Award winning Dallas TV reporter and author of the book, <u>*Free Publicity*</u>, wrote the following:

> "If you're one of those people who works countless hours building a strong product and about two seconds coming up with a name for it, there's a name for you: *naïve.*
>
> What you call your product or service may be even more important than how good it is. Just ask Dave Schwartz. His used car business was launched into the heavens by coming up with a name that would make many PR people faint. He called his company *Rent-A-Wreck.* Calling his cars what they were was pure marketing genius. The name brought Schwartz millions of

113

dollars in media exposure and an army of loyal frugal customers.

In the early 90's when the Dallas Cowboys and San Francisco 49'ers met in the NFL playoffs year after year, the cafe, *San Francisco Rose,* in Dallas would take advantage of a temporary name change to cash in on some free publicity. The Greenville Avenue eatery would announce to the local media that in honor of their Cowboys, they would be changing the name of the restaurant to the *"Dallas" Rose* in the week leading up to the big game. For several years in a row, every media outlet in Dallas covered the news event in which they draped a *"Dallas"* banner over the *"San Francisco"* side of the sign. Obviously, they discovered that a rose by a different name could be very sweet indeed."

We live in an age of acronyms, initials and "in house" vocabulary. We must honestly ask, *"Do these catchy titles and names 'Share the Big Picture' with the clients we need to reach?"*
Several years ago, I did business with a sizable company in Houston that rented out all kinds of visual aids products. They adopted the initials, *AIDS* in all advertising. It was on all delivery trucks, invoices and signage. I don't need to tell you that as the *Acquired Immune Deficiency Syndrome* began to spread, this company had to go through a total identification make-over.

My advice is make sure your company name helps to clearly *"Share the Big Picture"* with your market.

 TEST

What do the INITIALS of these ten world-renown companies stand for and what is the main thrust of their business? If you get 7 out of the 10 correct you pass!

- ➢ IBM
- ➢ AT&T
- ➢ BBB
- ➢ 3M
- ➢ AOL
- ➢ HP
- ➢ KPMG LLP
- ➢ NASDAQ
- ➢ MBNA
- ➢ UPS

(Answers at the end of this chapter)

If you had trouble with these well-known abbreviations, think about how *the name* of your company or product shares its purpose and story with your market.

Your business card should *"Share the Big Picture"*! It should have all the needed contact information, your name and position with the company, but it should also

115

answer this question, *"What is the vision and purpose of this company/product?"*

Follow the same guidelines regarding your name tag!

The most common mistake made in networking is having the attitude, *"They know me ..."*

Never take anything for granted and never forget:
<u>nothing sells itself!</u>

In a business networking and leadership environment be the Boy Scout, *"always prepared"* with:

> ➢ Business Cards
>
> ➢ Name Tag
>
> ➢ One Minute Commercial

In your own mind and in your organization the *"Big Picture"* needs to be renewed and updated constantly and adjusted according to the audience. There is always a tendency to wander away from the basics. Remember the famous NFL coach, Vince Lombardy, and his first meeting with the Green Bay Packers? He began his remarks, with a football in his hands, by saying, *"Gentlemen, this is a football!"* From there he went on to thoroughly coach the football basics ... blocking, tackling and running. Nothing works like executing the basics perfectly in football and business leadership networking.

The synonym for the ninth commandment, *"Share the Big Picture"* is <u>VISION</u>. A leader must be able to cast the vision and tell the story.

<u>*ADDITIONAL WISDOM FOR THE NINTH COMMANDMENT*</u>

SHARE THE BIG PICTURE

"Big results require big ambitions."
James Champy, *management coach*

"Every man takes the limits of his own field of vision for the limits of the world."
Arthur Schopenhauer,

"Hype is the awkward and desperate attempt to convince journalists that what you've made is worth the misery of having to review it."
Federico Fellini, *movie director*

"Winner: Someone who recognizes his God-given talents, works his tail off to develop them into skills, and uses these skills to accomplish his goals."
Larry Bird, *NBA player and coach*

"Your vision will become clear only when you look into your heart. Who looks outside, dreams. Who looks inside, awakens."
                    Carl Jung, *Swiss psychologist & psychiatrist*

"If people don't like us, they don't like us, but at least they have heard the story."
                    Lee Scott, *Wal-Mart CEO*

EMPOWERING YOUR
ONE MINUTE COMMERCIAL

The Key Ingredients in a 60 Second Networking Commercial

In most networking situations you have only a few seconds to get the necessary information to your prospective client. How can that be done easily and naturally while being concise, clear and personable?

1. You must be willing to step out of your *comfort zone* a little! Smile, speak to others and compliment them. Usually you will get a wonderful response!

2. Realize what your 60 second commercial is about! It's not about hiding your value! It's about introducing yourself and your company! It's about telling your story, and only you can do that! It's about first impressions!

3. Always practice your commercial and test it by asking these six key questions. Does it answer: *Who? What? Where? When? Why? and How?*

4. **GREAT** one minute commercials will answer three basic questions:

   1) *WHAT is your business?*
      (Get back in touch with WHAT you do, and stay in touch with it. Learn new and fresh ways to "cast the vision" about WHAT you do.)

   2) *WHO is your customer?*
      (WHO uses your product or service? Define your market! Identify who you need to reach! Paint a word picture of your ideal client or prospect.)

   3) *What does your CUSTOMER VALUE?*
      (How do you serve the customer or client what he needs, and how does he get value service and benefit from it? Describe what you do for your client and share what's in it for him.)

 You have been given a one minute commercial on national TV! It's free! Millions will see and hear you! The question the interviewer has asked you is, *"What about your company? Tell us your story!"*

This is your opportunity of a life time! **WHAT WILL YOU SAY?**

Your one minute commercial is just this vital. It's the most important speech you will ever give!

ANSWERS TO THE "TEST" ABOUT FAMOUS COMPANIES THEIR REAL NAMES AND WHAT THEY DO:

IBM - *International Business Machines*
They started out in typewriters and have evolved into computers, electronic communications, international call centers, technology... etc.

AT&T - *American Telephone and Telegraph*
While the telegraph is long gone and the telephone has evolved, in many cases, into a wireless communication device that can include a computerized entertainment center with multiple uses, the capacity of this company has far surpassed the original sphere its name suggests.

BBB - *Better Business Bureau*
Membership in this organization builds credibility and trustworthiness to a business.

3M - *Minnesota Mining and Manufacturing*
From early years of mining and manufacturing, this company has evolved into all kinds of office products, electronics and insulation with the auto industry as their main focus.

AOL - *America Online Time Warner*
The world's largest media enterprise comprised of at least six major communication companies.

HP - *Hewlett-Packard*
Now a world wide company which deals in computer technology.

KPMG LLP - *Klynveld, Peat, Marwick & Goerdeler*
One of the big five professional service organizations in financial services, consulting, taxes, assurance, banking, etc ---100,000 employees, in over 820 cities and 159 countries around the world.

Nasdaq - *National Association of Securities Dealers Automated Quotations System*
Here the name of the company just about says it all. "Nasdaq" is a national association of securities dealers where stocks are traded through an automated quotations system.

MBNA - *MBNA America Bank NA*
The largest independent credit card issuer in the world, that handles loans of nearly $80 billion.

UPS - *United Parcel Services, Inc.*
The world's largest express carrier and package delivery company, delivering more than 12 million packages each day to more then 200 countries.

Handouts for Commandment Nine
are on the next two pages.

`

**A LEADER'S NINTH
COMMANDMENT**

"SHARE THE BIG PICTURE"

**Dr. Shirley Neely, Secretary of Education
for the State of Texas, says,**

*"Sometimes you have to tell your own
story! You're the only one who can!"*

"The Big Picture" **is the overall goal and purpose of
your business, your position or your product**

**In helping others to see the whole picture some say too
_____ and some say too _____.**

"THE BIG PICTURE"
IS HOW <u>YOU</u> SEE IT— YOUR VISION!

Perhaps the biggest challenge of all is to *"Share the Big
Picture"* **about your company, organization or product**
in one sentence.

THE COMPANY _____
CAN *"SHARE THE BIG PICTURE"*

**We live in an age of acronyms, initials and
"in house" vocabulary. We must honestly
ask,** *"Do these catchy titles and names
'Share the Big Picture' with the clients we
need to reach?"*

Your business card should *"Share the Big Picture"*! It should have all the needed contact information, your name and position with the company, but it should also answer this question, *"What is the vision and purpose of this company/product?"*

Never take anything for granted and never forget:

_____ *sells itself!*

In a business networking and leadership environment be the Boy Scout, *"always prepared"* with:

- ➢ **Business Cards**
- ➢ **Name Tag**
- ➢ **One Minute Commercial**

The synonym for the ninth commandment, *"Share the Big Picture"* is <u>VISION</u>.

A leader must be able to cast the vision and tell the story.

COMMANDMENT #10

You Reap
What You Sow

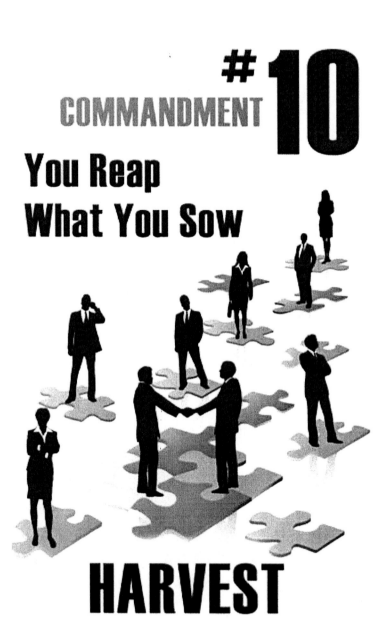

HARVEST

A LEADER'S TENTH
COMMANDMENT

YOU REAP WHAT YOU SOW

The first eighteen years of my life I was a farm boy.
Yes, it is true, *"You can take a boy out of the country, but
you can't take the country out of a boy."* Many who read
these words have a rural background through your
parents or grandparents. There among the soil and
farm life we learn truths about life and success.

We learn to work with the great laws the Creator has
placed in the earth. These laws are undeniable,
unbreakable and unchangeable, such as *The Law of
Gravity.* This law works no matter who is involved. If
the Queen of England is pushed from The Tower of
London, she will fall to the surface below ... no matter
how rich, powerful, loved, educated or what ... the law
of gravity will work!

There is another law which is just as sure as the law of
gravity, it is *The Law of Seedtime and Harvest.* It cannot
fail!

After Noah's flood, with the rainbow came the promise,
"As long as the earth endures, seedtime and harvest, cold

and heat, summer and winter, day and night will never cease." (Genesis 8:22)
Paul, the Apostle, simply states the law in these words, *"...YOU REAP WHAT YOU SOW." (Galatians 6:7)*

This is a wonderful positive law. Because it is true, we have food to eat, clothes to wear, homes to live in and a livelihood.

 This undeniable and unchangeable law of harvest is sometimes called *"The Law of Giving and Receiving".*

Zig Ziglar's well known way of wording it is, *"You can have everything in life you want, if you will just help enough other people get what they want!"*

It is as sure and dependable as the law of gravity, and it applies to your everyday business life.

This has also been called *The Law of Multiplication!*

George Bernard Shaw, the writer, put it this way, *"If you have an apple and I have an apple, and we exchange these apples, then you and I have one apple each. But if you have an IDEA and I have an IDEA, and we exchange these IDEAS, each of us will have TWO IDEAS!"*

The multiplication factor in networking and team building is tremendous. It pays off in many ways for many people.

THREE BASIC FACTS ABOUT THE LAW OF HARVEST - MULTIPLICATION

1. You Reap *WHAT* you sow!

It can't happen any other way!

➢ You will reap IN KIND! If you plant wheat, corn, cotton, rice, beans or peas, you can only get what you planted. Don't expect anything but the type of seed you planted.

➢ You will reap IN QUANTITY! If you plant a few seeds or many seeds, much or little, dense or sparse, that's how the increase will come.

➢ You will reap IN QUALITY! If the seed is common or hybrid, regular or mixed, you will reap according to the grade and excellence of the seeds.

2. You Reap *AFTER* you sow!

It can't happen any other way! Until the seed is sown, it can not be multiplied!

➢ Receiving follows our giving! Sow first and harvest follows!

➢ Sow the seed for the harvest you desire or for the equivalent benefit!

➢ After sowing there is a time of patiently cultivating, watering, weeding and care, before the production comes.

3. You Reap _MORE_ _THAN_ you sow!

It can't happen any other way!
It's the law of multiplication!

➤ How many seeds are needed
for one stalk of corn or
wheat? ONE! It takes only
one seed per stalk! How
many grains of corn or wheat come from one
stalk? Hundreds!

➤ Now this is exciting! This is seedtime and
HARVEST! Reaping a bumper crop!

The law of harvest says, _You Reap WHAT you sow,_
AFTER you sow and MORE THAN you sow!

YES, BUT HOW? ...

HOW CAN IT HAPPEN
IN YOUR LIFE?

In networking for your business, what are the seeds you
must sow?

✓ A smile, friendly greeting and handshake!

✓ Be generous with your business cards, letters,
calls and advertisements! Sow generously!

✓ Render heartfelt service! Meet needs! Share
leads and referrals!

✓ Sincerely help others solves their problems!

Say to yourself as you do these things, *"I am sowing seeds!"*

Then ask, *"How can I cultivate and water the seeds sown?"*

Then, anticipate a harvest and be ready to gather it!

What kind of harvest do you need? Sow seeds that would bring that harvest! SOW! Everything produces after its kind!

EVERY TIME YOU HARVEST REMEMBER THREE THINGS:

1) Save some of the seeds to sow again!

2) Put some in storage (savings) for hard times!

3) Enjoy and "spend" some of the seeds!

Plan your harvest! Sow what you want to reap!

The law of harvest will not fail!

Our one word synonym for the tenth commandment, *"You Reap What You Sow"*, is the word <u>HARVEST</u>!

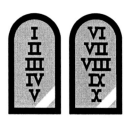

ADDITIONAL WISDOM FOR THE TENTH COMMANDMENT:

YOU REAP WHAT YOU SOW

"If you don't like what you are getting, change what you are doing."

Author unknown

"Down the fairway of life, smell the roses, for you only get to play one round."

Ben Hogan, *golfer*

"To acquire knowledge, one must study. But to acquire wisdom, one must observe."

Marilyn vos Savant, *writer*

"No one would have crossed the ocean if he could have gotten off the ship in the storm."

Charles Kettering, *inventor*

"The most prepared are the most dedicated."

Raymond Berry, *NFL player, coach*

"Opportunity rarely knocks on your door. Knock rather on opportunity's door if you wish to enter."
B.C. Forbes, *publisher*

"Small deeds done are better than great deeds planned."
Peter Marshall, *U.S. Senate chaplain*

"Alone we can do so little. Together we can do so much."
Helen Keller, *lecturer*

"Baseball is the only field of endeavor where a man can succeed three times out of 10 and be considered a good performer."
Ted Williams, *baseball player*

"Success is neither magical nor mysterious. Success is the natural consequences of consistently applying the basic fundamentals."
Jim Rohn, *motivational speaker*

"Personal excellence can be achieved by a visionary goal, thorough planning, dedicated execution and total follow-through."
Gerald Ford, *38th U.S. president*

"Be nice to people on your way up because you meet them on your way down."
Jimmy Durante, *actor*

"What kills a skunk is the publicity it gives itself."
Abraham Lincoln, *16th* U.S. president

"Cast your bread upon the waters, for after many days you will find it again."
Solomon, *Ecclesiastes 11:1*

What you put into the life of others comes back!

One day a teacher asked her students to list the names of the other students in the classroom on two sheets of paper, leaving a space between each name.

Then she told them to think of the nicest thing they could say about each of their classmates and write it down. It took the remainder of the class period to finish the assignment, and as the students left the room, each one handed in the papers.

That weekend, the teacher wrote down the name of each student on a separate sheet of paper, and listed what everyone else had said about that individual.

On Monday she gave each student his or her list. Before long, the entire class was smiling. "Really?" she heard whispered. "I never knew that I meant anything to anyone!" and, "I didn't know others liked me so much," were most of the comments.

No one ever mentioned those papers in the class again. She never knew if they discussed them after class or with their parents, but it didn't matter. The exercise had accomplished its purpose. The students were happy with themselves and one another. That group of students moved on.

Several years later, one of the students was killed in Viet Nam, and his teacher attended the funeral of that special student. She had never seen a serviceman in a military coffin before. He looked so handsome, so mature.

The church was packed with his friends. One by one those who loved him walked by the coffin. The teacher was the last one to pass by. As she stood there, one of the soldiers who acted as pallbearer came up to her. "Were you Mark's math teacher?" he asked. She nodded: "Yes." Then he said, "Mark talked about you a lot."

After the funeral, most of Mark's former classmates went together to a luncheon. Mark's mother and father were there, obviously waiting to speak with his teacher.

"We want to show you something," his father said, taking a wallet out of his pocket, "They found this on Mark when he was killed. We thought you might recognize it."

Opening the billfold, he carefully removed two worn pieces of notebook paper that had obviously been taped, folded and refolded many times. The teacher knew without looking that the papers were the ones on which she had listed all the good things each of Mark's classmates had said about him.

"Thank you so much for doing that," Mark's mother said. "As you can see, Mark treasured it."

All of Mark's former classmates started to gather around. Charlie smiled rather sheepishly and said, "I still have my list. It's in the top drawer of my desk at home." Chuck's wife said, "Chuck asked me to put his in our wedding album." "I have mine too," Marilyn said. "It's in my diary." Then Vicki, another classmate, reached in her purse, took out her wallet and showed her worn and frazzled list to the group. "I carry this with me at all times," Vicki said and without batting an eyelash, she continued, "I think we all saved our lists."

That's when the teacher finally sat down and cried. She cried for Mark and for all his friends and family ... but a warm feeling of love and care filled each heart!

Celeste Holm, the great actress, said, "We live by encouragement and die without it – slowly, sadly, angrily.

So please, tell the people you love and care for, that they are special and important. Tell them! It will reap a great harvest of encouragement!

Remember, you reap what you sow. What you put into the lives of others comes back into your own.

Jim Pratt, *encourager*

A LEADER'S TENTH COMMANDMENT

YOU REAP WHAT YOU SOW

(Seedtime & Harvest)

The undeniable, unbreakable and unchangeable LAW OF HARVEST is the 10th Commandment, sometimes called THE LAW OF GIVING & RECEIVING.

Zig Ziglar's version is, *"You can have everything in life you want, if you will just help enough other people get what they want."* It's as sure and dependable as THE LAW OF GRAVITY, and it applies to your everyday business life.

THREE BASIC FACTS ABOUT THE LAW OF HARVEST

1. You reap _____ you sow! – *It can't happen any other way!*
   * You reap *in kind!*
   * You reap *in quality!*
   * You reap *in quantity!*

2. You reap _____ you sow! – *It can't happen any other way!*
   * You sow *first* and *harvest* follows!
   * You sow *seed* for the harvest you desire!
   * You sow and then *care* for the plant!

3. You reap _____ _____ you sow! – *It can't happen any other way!*

YES, BUT HOW? ... HOW CAN IT HAPPEN IN YOUR BUSINESS LIFE?

➤ What are the *seeds* you must sow in your business to get results?

➤ Say to yourself as you do these things, *"I am sowing seeds!"*

➤ Then ask, *"How can I cultivate and water the seeds sown?"*

➤ Then anticipate a *harvest* and *be ready to gather it!*

EVERY TIME YOU HARVEST, REMEMBER THREE THINGS:

1) Save some seed *to sow again!*

2) Put some in storage (savings) *for hard times!*

3) *Enjoy* and "spend" some of the seeds!

Plan your harvest!   Sow what you want to reap!

THE LAW OF HARVEST WILL NOT FAIL!

Our one word synonym for the tenth commandment is

HARVEST!

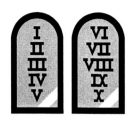

Ten Commandments of Leadership Networking

Summary:

COMMANDMENT	Key Word:
1. Always a host, never a guest.	SERVICE
2. Never underestimate the applause of one.	SUPPORT
3. Expect change and be flexible.	VERSITILITY
4. Trust is the foundation.	CHARACTER
5. Wherever you are, be all there.	FOCUS
6. People are usually down on what they are not up on.	COMMUNICATION
7. Timing is everything.	FLOW
8. People do what people see.	MODEL
9. Share the big picture.	VISION
10. You reap what you sow.	HARVEST

These TEN COMMANDMENTS will help you:

- ➤ get out of a mental rut.
- ➤ have creative thoughts.
- ➤ acquire a new outlook.
- ➤ fire new ambitions.

You will build lasting and valuable friendships and increase your influence and your ability to get things done.

Your earning power will increase because you will win new clients and customers. As you arouse enthusiasm among your associates with new people skills, you will also be able to coach and train others.

You will become a better presenter and conversationalist.

Acknowledgements

A special word of thanks to the following (only a partial listing) who have attended "BRANCH OUT", a weekly networking group of the Farmers Branch Chamber of Commerce, or other groups where the <u>Ten Commandments of Leadership Networking</u> were presented.

Jesse Abercrombie
Edward Jones

Fred Badyna
Estate & Retirement Consultant

Wayne Baham
Advocates Realty

Charlie Bird
Bird's Hardwood Floors

Cia Bond
Metrocrest Medical Foundation

Richard Brown
New York Life

Chuck McKenny
Edward Jones

Joe Catalona
Joe's Italian Café

John Custer
Banners & Signs, etc

Bobby Drake
Brookhaven Country Club Barber

Dr. Janie Hodges
Valley View Pet Health Center

Daren Horton
Gecko Pest Control

Syd Kazmi
Ink-R-Cycle

Bill Moses
Metrocrest Sales

Joyce Nissen
Doubletree Club Hotel

Michael Northway
Blue Elephant Promotions

Lara Orlic
Farmers Branch Chamber of Commerce

Bob Phelps
Mayor of Farmers Branch

Keith Martino
Sales Training & Leadership Workshops

Floyd Prather
Unified Tek

Mike Lovell
EmbroidMe

Jim Pratt
Worker's Comp Alternatives

Jeff Richardson
Special Interest Automotive

Ralph Taylor
Chase Printing & Graphics

Warren Witt
Budget Blinds

Jason O'Quinn
Petra Lending Group

Ryan Nienstadt
Abrock Pest Management

Tammi Burgee
Fidelity National Home Warranty

C.W. Lowrimore
Tex – Tenn. Transporters

Cheryl Edwards & Donna Steindorf
Your Federal Credit Union

Mike Loustaunau
State Farm

James McDonald
Ambit Energy

Anne Acuna
Bentley Manor

Charles Dupar
Sam's Club Business Development

Aaron Cottle
The Master's Press

Bob Baxter
Ignite Energy

Matt Bednarz
Legacy Retirement Solutions

Bryan Sanders
Cobalt Surveillance

Tamela Johnson
A Link – for – Life

Nicole Bennett & Jay Willis
Star Medical Group

Sonny Hastings
Legacy Lending

David Patterson
Las Colinas Re/Max

Ted Snow
Snow Financial Group

Gincy Hartin
Dallas Christian College

Kurt Horn
Texas Lending Solutions

Don Braugh
Brookhaven Country Club –
Tennis

Larry Bartlett
Account – CPA

Bill Priestley
Saxby's Coffee

Jeff Weaver
Ebby Halliday Realtors

Sue Brown
Dobson Floors

Theron Russell
FASTSIGNS of Carrollton

Dan Barrios
Marshall's Bar-B-Que

Rick Robson
MinuteMan Press

Sandee Treptow
Reliant Energy

Eric Brown
Texans Can Academy

Debbi Witt
Farmers Branch Chamber of
Commerce

Brett Parsley
Ebby Halliday Realtors

Phil Bergman
Bergman's Paint & Body, Inc.

Larry Kramer
Mobility Solutions of Texas

Dr. Robert Peretti
Chiropractor

Edwin Evidente & Louis
Prada
Capital One

Lawrence Dsouza
H & R BLOCK

Rose M. Bryan
Bryan Realty

W. Bruce Woody
Attorney at Law

Tom Fry
Keller Williams Realty

Gail Funderburk
Neighbors GO

Kent Hankins
Kite Networks, Inc.

About the Author

Eddy Ketchersid

3001 Randy Lane
Farmers Branch (Dallas), TX 75234

Home: 972-241-0510
Office: 972-247-2109
Cell: 972-345-1645

Email:
broeddy@thebranch.org
eketchersid@thebranch.org

EDMOND (EDDY) RAY KETCHERSID

RESUME

Born: November 28, 1936, Hardeman County Texas
(Quanah, TX. is the County seat)

Parents: Owen & Bessie Ketchersid;
Sisters: Ruby Nell Loe & Nancy E. Brown

Education:

Various Church Growth, Small Group & Leadership
Seminars/Workshops

ABILENE CHRISTIAN UNIVERSITY – Bachelor of
Arts Degree, Bible & Speech, May 25, 1959

AMARILLO COLLEGE – Liberal Arts Associates
Degree, May 30, 1957

AMARILLO BIBLE TRAINING WORK Seminary
2-year Degree, May 15, 1957

CROWELL HIGH SCHOOL – Graduation, May 20, 1955

Ordained: Ordained Minister of the Gospel, July 24, 1957, by Elders of West Amarillo Church Of Christ, Amarillo, TX.

Married: Verlen (Hayes), August 31, 1957

Children: Six – 3 sons, 3 daughters: Allen, Karla (Kindberg), Tim, John, Elizabeth (Denn), Vivian (Smith) All married; 25 grandchildren.

Ministry: Farmers Branch Church of Christ, Farmers Branch (Dallas), TX. 1988 – present.

Main St. Church of Christ, South Houston, TX. 1959 – 1987, 28 years.

Palm St. Church of Christ, Abilene, TX., 1957 – 1959, 2 years.

(2 sons and 2 sons-in-law are ordained ministers: Allen Ketchersid, Indiana; John Ketchersid Ft. Worth, Texas; Stuart Smith Turkey, Texas; Tony Denn, Oregon.)

Organizations:

Farmers Branch Chamber of Commerce, 1988 – present (Executive Board member Founder & Chairman of Ambassadors Club & *Teaches "Networking"* .

Metrocrest Chamber of Commerce. (Metrocrest Citizen Of The Year 2002)

Coppell Chamber of Commerce.

Carrollton -Farmers Branch ISD Educational Foundation, Charter Board member.

Metrocrest Ministers Fellowship, 1988 – present.

Metrocrest Mayors' Prayer Breakfast Committee (Founder, 1990).

Rotary Club, Farmers Branch, 2002 - present

Red Ribbon Breakfast Committee, Chairman 15 years.

Honorary Life Membership, PTA

(Various organizations and committees served in Houston before moving to Dallas)

Honors: Metrocrest (Farmers Branch, Carrollton, Addison)
Citizen of Year – 2002

Present Position:

COMMUNITY MINISTER, Farmers Branch Church of Christ, 3035 Valley View Lane, Farmers Branch (Dallas), TX. 75234

CHAPLAIN, City of Farmers Branch.

Also available from Eddy Ketchersid:

Networking Nuggets is a great resource for business people and leaders who want to enhance their skills for connecting well with others.

The book includes 15 presentations that you can use to motivate and inspire others in your organization.

Available from:

Ketch Publishing

812-327-0072

www.KetchPublishing.com